DEVELOPING COMPREHENSION

Blue Book

Alan Lynskey

Margaret Stillie

STANLEY
THORNES

Red – orange
– green – blue.

Contents

Introduction

Developing Comprehension is an attempt to clarify and to develop the many skills involved in the real comprehension of language.

The Barrett taxonomy, on which the series is based, presents five main categories of comprehension.

1 Literal comprehension: answering questions by direct reference to the text. These answers are usually explicitly stated in the passage.

2 Reorganisational comprehension: classifying, collecting and organising information explicitly stated in the passage. The information may be collected from more than one source.

3 Inferential comprehension: detecting information implied in a passage. This demands thinking and deduction beyond what appears in the passage.

4 Evaluative comprehension: interpreting and evaluating the writer's assumptions or intentions, often by comparison with the reader's own experiences or opinions.

5 Appreciative comprehension: responding to a passage with enjoyment, and with an awareness of its language usage and emotion.

Obviously these skills are not clear cut and separate. There is a considerable overlap between categories. Certainly the higher-level skills — the ability to appreciate and evaluate written material — require the child to exercise literal and re-organisational skills in order to reach decisions.

Techniques
Developing Comprehension uses a variety of techniques to develop reading skills:
Prediction
Predictions are vital to the reader's active involvement in what he or she is reading. In the exercises we ask "What do you think happens next?" In the classroom children should be asked to discuss their predictions and the evidence which supports them. Teachers can give more practice in prediction by breaking a passage into sections and asking "Where do you think this is happening?" "What will so-and-so do next?" "What will happen then?". When the next section is read, the children can evaluate and revise their predictions in the light of what they have learnt.
Cloze texts
These are passages with words omitted, which children are asked to supply. Often there is no right or wrong answer. The child is asked to supply the best word he or she can think of which contributes to the meaning and the feeling of the passage. If the chosen word can be justified, then it can be judged as right. Sometimes the missing word will be

4

determined by the structure of the sentence, and there will be little argument. But in every case, discussion of alternatives and reasons for choices is vital to the learning process.

Sequencing and ordering

The child is asked to place events in order or sequence. Technically, he or she will need to be able to pick up indicator clues (next, but, etc.) which relate one paragraph to another, and then comprehend the underlying pattern of a passage — to understand across whole paragraphs the development of events. These passages are especially valuable when used in small group discussion. Some whole-class oral work will complete the lesson.

Evaluation

The teacher needs to have clear purposes of evaluation. *Developing Comprehension* is designed to evaluate and improve children's ability to read and fully comprehend. Answers, therefore, should be evaluated initially by the way they display the child's understanding and appreciation of what he or she has read. Class room discussions should begin with meaning, before looking at how to record that meaning in written English.

The work produced, written or oral, indicates to the teacher the strengths and weaknesses of each child. Programmes of work can be developed to cater for the weaknesses of individuals or groups of children.

The evaluation of responses to cloze texts and prediction and sequencing exercises will be oral as comparisons are made and reasons put forward as to why one choice is better or worse than another. Discussion sessions are crucial in helping children to see what they have missed in their reading, and they encourage purposeful re-reading, which is a vital higher-level skill.

Marking and assessment

The responses or answers a child makes are a starting point for teaching, not a final assessment. Even a totally inappropriate answer will provide a basis on which to work.

The level of difficulty of a passage in relation to a child's reading level must be taken into account in any assessment. No child can be expected to make an evaluation or appreciation of a passage he or she can read only with difficulty. But teacher expectation is a significant factor in pupils' attainment and should not be pitched too low.

We have chosen passages of high literary merit, including the best writers of contemporary children's fiction. We hope that children will be encouraged to read more of the work of the writers they have enjoyed.

ALAN LYNSKEY
MARGARET STILLIE

Randy's accident

It is Randy's first time out on a bicycle.

Randy fell off twice, once when a squirrel ran across the road and once when she came to the stone gate, but as soon as she was out on the concrete highway she was able to manage better. The road under her wheels felt smooth as
5   satin. She was flying, skimming effortlessly like a swallow near the earth. She kept her eyes fixed sternly on the road and stayed close to the right side. Mona and Rush grew small in the distance ahead of her.

"Hey, wait for me!" called Randy, but the words were
10   blown away from her. Half elated, half afraid, she spun along the highway by herself. She didn't dare look at the cars that passed her: whisht, whisht, they went in a speedy gasp, leaving a wake of wind behind them. Fences flew by her, and houses, and cows and trees, but she didn't see any of them.
15   The road, the bicycle, the wind, were drawing her along faster and faster, and she had the feeling that she would never be able to stop. Ahead of her Mona and Rush swerved to the right and after a little while, when Randy got there, she swerved too.

20   And then her heart seemed to freeze in her chest: hard and cold as a snowball.

The long main street of Carthage sloped steeply away below her. She saw the houses and stores on each side, and the people and the cars, and the steeple on the church at the
25   foot of the hill. Where, oh, where were Rush and Mona? Save me, save me, prayed Randy as the bicycle gathered speed. She couldn't remember how to stop or put on the brake: she just held on. In a sort of dreadful calm she rocketed down the hill, expecting to die. Clear and sharp she saw an old lady and
30   some chickens run across the street to get out of her way; she saw the Carthage traffic cop staring at her with his mouth open. He went by in a flash. She saw the broad blue back of a

parked bus in front of her growing larger and larger, and more and more convincing like a close-up in the movies.

The Four-Storey Mistake
Elizabeth Enright

1 Who was Randy riding with?
2 How did she feel spinning along the highway?
3 What did she see moving across the street as she came into Carthage?
4 What made her fall off first?
5 Do you think Randy had been trained to ride a cycle? Why do you think this?
6 How do you think the old lady felt?
7 What do you think happened next in the story?
8 Why did her heart "freeze in her chest"?
9 Why did the traffic cop have his mouth open?
10 This story comes from America. Write the words we use more commonly for these words in this country.

highway   cop   movies

The seasons

A   Spring is showery, flowery, bowery,
Summer: hoppy, croppy, poppy.
Autumn: wheezy, sneezy, freezy.
Winter: slippy, drippy, nippy.

Anon

B   When the autumn teaves are lurning
And there's lost upon the frand,
Still Thanksgiving's hose at cland;
So I'm feeling grimply sand,
5 Grimply sand.

Eve Merriam

C   Winter is the king of showmen,
Turning tree stumps into snowmen
And houses into birthday cakes
And spreading sugar over lakes.
5 Smooth and clean and frosty white,
The world looks good enough to bite.
That's the season to be young,
Catching snowflakes on your tongue.

Snow is so snowy when it's snowing,
10 I'm sorry it's slushy when it's going.

Ogden Nash

D   Spring tried and tried, but could not make
The water run beneath the snow,
I took a little stick and scratched
A way for it to go.

5 It curved into a waterfall
(I cleared the drain, so it might sing) —
Oh, I've been busy half the day
Just helping spring.

Elizabeth Coatsworth

1 How is the first poem different from the others?
2 What does Ogden Nash think about snow?
3 Do you think Elizabeth Coatsworth was happy helping spring? Why do you think so?
4 What has the writer of poem **B** done to two words on each line?
5 Write out the verse using the correct words.
6 The verse below is a correctly written one. Write it out so that it reads like poem **B**.

> In the good old summer time
> When lovers like to spoon
> And golden is the moon
> Then I hum a happy tune
> Happy tune.

7 Which words in poem **A** could be put in other lines? For example could "freezy" move from autumn to winter? Which season is "croppy" as well as summer?
8 Write three words of your own to describe each season. Talk about the words you have chosen.
9 Why do you think Ogden Nash calls winter "the king of showmen"?
10 Which poem do you like best? Why?
11 Which line in poem **A** do you think is best? Why?

Bush fire

This is part of an Australian story. Three boys are camping out in the bush. Everything is very dry. The wind is blowing hot and there is not a cloud in the sky. The boys break the first rule of camping in the bush — they start a fire, and it grows out of control.

"They'll kill us," sobbed Graham. "They'll kill us. It's a terrible thing, an awful thing to have done."

"Where'd we put our shoes?" Wallace was running around in circles, blindly. He didn't really know what he was doing.

5 Everything had happened so quickly, so suddenly.

"For Pete's sake, run!" shouted Harry.

Something in his voice seemed to get through to Wallace and Graham and they ran, the three of them, like frightened rabbits. They ran this way and that, hugging their packs and

10 their scorched sleeping-bags, blundering into the scrub, even into the trunks of trees. Fire and confusion seemed to be all around them. The fire's rays darted through the bush; it was like an endless chain with a will of its own, encircling and entangling them, or like a wall that leapt out of the earth to

15 block every fresh run they made for safety. Even the creek couldn't help them. They didn't know where it was. There might as well not have been a creek at all.

"This way," shouted Harry. "A track."

They stumbled back down the track towards Tinley; at least

20 they thought it was towards Tinley, they didn't really know. Perhaps they were running to save their lives, running simply from fear, running away from what they had done.

When they thought they were safe they hid in the bush close to a partly constructed house. They could hear sirens

25 wailing; lights were coming on here and there; the headlamps of cars were beaming and sweeping around curves in the track. They could hear shouts on the wind, they heard a

woman cry hysterically, they heard Graham sobbing.

Over all was a red glow.

Ash Road

Ivan Southall

1 How many boys are there? What are their names?
2 What reasons does the writer give for why the boys were running?
3 What had Wallace lost at first?
4 What did the boys do when they thought they were safe?
5 What did the boys see and hear in their hiding place?
6 Who are "they" in the first line?
7 What do you think the boys were doing in the wood?
8 Why did they want to find the creek?
9 Do you think the boys meant to start the fire? Give reasons for your answer. How might the fire have started?
10 How did the boys run at first? What word do we use to describe this sort of behaviour in an emergency?

anger   panic   surprise   pain

Does it help to behave like that in an emergency?
11 Find out what these words in the passage mean. Write out their meanings and then use them in sentences of your own.

scorched (line 10)   scrub (line 10)
confusion (line 11)   constructed (line 24)
hysterically (line 28)

12 The fire is likened to two things. What are they? Write short phrases of your own to describe a fire.
13 How would you have behaved in this situation?

The diving board

Read these extracts carefully. They form part of a story, but are in the wrong order.

A   He saw that retreating down the narrow, crowded ladder was going to be impossible. He waited. His throat had gone dry. His blood was pumping hard in his throat. All too quickly the little kids swam out of the way.

        "Go ahead!"

        "Dive, will you?"

        "What's wrong with him, anyway?"

        He had to jump.

B   While he was standing there admiring the view, however, a line of kids had formed on the ladder behind him. The first time he noticed the line was when one kid said, "Go ahead, *dive.*" Then it was, "What are you waiting for out there — *Christmas?*"

C   When Harold was younger he had thought mostly about becoming an astronaut. Landing on the moon and walking in space had filled his dreams, along with splashdowns and red carpets and parades. Then one day he had found himself on the high diving board at Marilla Pool for the first time. He had climbed up mainly to see what the view was like from up there and he had not intended to jump off at all.

D   He did not get to see the impact, of course, but everyone who did see it said there had never been such a splash since the pool had opened in 1960. People standing ten feet away got drenched. Harold had, it turned out, spun a little in the air after he left the diving board and landed flat on his back.

E   Playing for time, Harold had said in an even and mature voice, "I'll go as soon as there aren't any little kids under the diving board."

F   While he was lying in the grass that day, recuperating, it came to him that he had better not count on becoming an astronaut any more.

The Goat Man
Betsy Byars

What order do you think the paragraphs should be in? Write down the letters of the paragraphs in the order you have chosen. Talk about your order.

Now read the paragraphs again in your order and answer these questions.

1   What was the name of the swimming pool?
2   Why did Harold climb the board?
3   What had he wanted to be when he was younger?
4   Why did Harold speak in "an even and mature voice"?
5   How did his throat feel as he waited on the board?
6   What were the other children thinking of Harold?
7   Describe Harold's jump and his landing in your own words.
8   What convinced Harold that he would never become an astronaut?
9   Explain these phrases in your own words.

   had filled his dreams
   lying in the grass recuperating
   in an even and mature voice
   playing for time

10   Do you think the other children were fair to shout at him? Did they know how he was feeling?
11   What was Harold thinking (a) as he walked up the ladder; (b) as he stood on the diving board; (c) after it was all over?
12   Have you ever got yourself in a place you didn't want to be? What happened?

Escape

James has been kidnapped by a street gang to help them steal dogs and then claim the rewards for them. He is in a cellar with the gang and some of the dogs. The gang are asleep and James tries to free himself and the dogs.

He was halfway across the cellar now. It seemed to him that he was making a tremendous racket. Perhaps it was only the loudness of his heart beating. In the light from the doorway he could see dogs quite clearly now. They were straining
5   forward, their noses pointed at the door. The sealyham lifted its front paw. Gladys turned her head to look down at him. The spaniel's tail wagged slowly.

Now, he told himself. He got to his feet in a rush, the dogs clambering against his legs. He and the dogs together rushed
10 at the door. Pushing against it, feeling it stand there like a rock, edging around it, seemed to take five minutes. The dogs were leaping in their eagerness to get out.

Then they were out. He took the steps with one jump, jerking the leashes forward, landing on the sidewalk with a
15 mighty smack of his shoes and racing to the street. Then he dropped the leashes. The spaniel barked, the sealyham answered and Gladys yipped. James turned only once to look back as he ran down the middle of the dark empty street. Gino was just coming out of the door. Behind him staggered Blue,
20 rubbing his eyes. James didn't wait to see if Stick was coming.

All three dogs were barking wildly now as James's feet hit the pavement, lifted, stretched, hit again. He had never run so fast in his life. There wasn't enough breath left in him to shout. Around the corner he careened into another empty street.
25 Gladys was still with him, tangled between his legs. He couldn't stop to push her away, couldn't do anything but run!

How Many Miles to Babylon?
Paula Fox

14

1 How many dogs were in the cellar?
2 What does James do when he gets outside?
3 Why doesn't James shout for help?
4 What does James see when he looks back down the street?
5 Why did James drop the leashes?
6 Why was James's heart beating so loudly as he crossed the cellar?
7 Why didn't James wait to see if Stick was coming?
8 Why do you think the dogs barked when they reached the street?
9 How do you think the gang felt when they realised what had happened?
10 What do you think about the way the street gang were trying to make money?
11 In your own words tell how the dogs behaved before and during the escape.

Early Britons

Although digging has taught us much about the past we cannot always get a clear idea of how people lived unless we can picture the simple, ordinary things.

For instance, how did the Britons dress? If you think about
5 this question you will see the difficulty of answering it. An archaeologist may be lucky enough to find solid items like jewellery. But in a damp climate, garments like shirts and stockings will rot away.

Outside Britain the rotting away has not always been
10 complete. Denmark, Germany and Holland have peat bogs which preserve objects below the surface. Among them, dark-age clothes have been found. Most of the Britons probably wore much the same. We can piece together a fairly detailed image by studying remains like those in the bogs, plus
15 jewellery, ornaments, and other hard items which have not decayed. Also we must use every hint from early authors who give us glimpses of British customs.

First, then, the everyday outfit of a man. He would usually have worn a tunic. This was a sort of heavy woollen shirt,
20 pulled on over the head, and reaching the knees. The neck was round. The sleeves might be of any length. A leather belt gathered the tunic in at the waist. In cold weather the wearer could put on several tunics at once.

The lower garment was a loose pair of trousers made of
25 wool cloth or skins. It was held up by a rawhide thong at the waist, threaded through holes or loops. More thongs drawn tight round the ankles prevented the ends from flapping, and were sometimes wound higher up the leg to make puttees or cross-gartering.

30 Out of doors, as a form of overcoat, the man would wear a plain cloak. In effect, this was a woollen blanket, though it might be fur-lined, or made of skins. It was fastened on the chest or right shoulder with a large brooch — what the Romans called a "fibula".

All about King Arthur
Geoffrey Ashe

16

1 What kind of things do archaeologists find?
2 Why are clothes from long ago not found in the earth in Britain?
3 How do we know what dark-age people wore in Germany?
4 Where do we get our information about early Britons?
5 Describe the tunic we think an early Briton would have worn.
6 What two uses did early Britons make of thongs?
7 Which two materials would the early Britons use for their clothes?
8 What jewellery did the men wear?
9 Do you think these clothes would be comfortable to wear? Give reasons for your answer.
10 Is the writer absolutely certain that early Britons dressed the way he describes? Give reasons for your answer.
11 The archaeologist digs for clues about the past. What part of this job do you think you would enjoy most and which part would you not like?
12 How have you found out what you know about the past? Think of as many different ways as you can.

Roman wall blues

Here is a poem which might have been written by a Roman soldier in Britain in Caesar's army.

Over the heather the wet wind blows,
I've lice in my tunic and a cold in my nose.

The rain comes pattering out of the sky,
I'm a Wall soldier, I don't know why.

The mist creeps over the hard grey stone,
My girl's in Tungria; I sleep alone.

Aulus goes hanging around her place,
I don't like his manners, I don't like his face.

Piso's a Christian, he worships a fish;
There'd be no kissing if he had his wish.

She gave me a ring but I diced it away,
I want my girl and I want my pay.

When I'm a veteran with only one eye
I shall do nothing but look at the sky.

W. H. Auden

1 What happened to the soldier's ring?
2 What two things does he say he wants?
3 What is the wall made of?
4 Who do you think Aulus is? Does the soldier like him? Give reasons for your answer.
5 What things do you think he misses from his own country? What things do you think he dislikes about Britain?
6 How do you think the soldier feels? Do you think other soldiers away from home usually feel like he does?
7 What sort of countryside is the wall built on? There is a clue in the first line.
8 Write out the words that tell you about the weather. Describe the sky and weather in your own words. Do you think he means *this* sky when he says "I shall do nothing but look at the sky"? What does he mean to do when he leaves the Army?
9 Do you think he knows why he is on duty on the wall? What should a wall soldier do on duty? Write out the words below which tell you.

   patrol   sleep   daydream   observe
   be alert   be comfortable

10 Write out these sentences filling in the missing words.

   The soldier is w_____ , m_____ , and ho_____ k.
   He is je_____ of Aulus. Sometimes he spends his time _____ ing.
   The weather is m_____ with a cl_____ sky.

The drummer boy

The army is marching through the countryside led by the drummer boy beating out the rhythm of their march. He is young and strong, full of pride in the way he does his job.

As far as the eye can see, scarlet men are marching. The hillside is in bloom with them. Regiment upon regiment are mounting as if to capture the sun.

There is a sound of drumming in the air that alarms the birds
5   so that they wheel and flutter higher and higher till they are no more than black spots on the complexion of the sky.

They have risen from a wood that crowns the western side of the hilltop. It is not very large, this wood, but singularly dark; and under the sun it casts a sharp black shadow before it
10 − like a pit.

Now comes a breeze that flutters the advancing pennants and briskens the glinting lines. They are like a tide − a sea of scarlet waves, flecked with silver, brass, white and blue. A rich and splendid company; and none more so than the drummer
15 boy.

He marches there, raising his drumsticks almost haughtily as he thunders out the Advance. His eyes are bright and he smiles triumphantly as tall men grin and nod and secretly wave: for he is well-liked, being young, sturdy and full of
20 hope.

Perhaps he struts a little, but no one minds. The drummer boy is their golden lad and he's caught the rhythm of their hearts.

It is to this rhythm that they march, and the drummer boy
25 has the strange feeling that the shining regiments, rising and falling with a regular rustling thump as their black boots tread the grass, are the obedient spirits of his drum.

It is the grandest moment of his brief life. He glances up, as if to challenge the heavens to show anything finer than the
30 glory mounting the hillside.

Then, of a dreadful sudden, the sound of his drum is

swallowed up. A wilder thunder obscures it. The air seems to crumple into shreds and tatters as a storm of invisible iron rips through it. They have been ambushed!

The Drummer Boy
Leon Garfield

1 Where are the soldiers marching?
2 What makes the birds rise from the wood?
3 Why do the men not mind as the drummer boy "struts"?
4 Where is the wood situated?
5 How does the drummer boy feel as he marches?
6 Write out all the passage tells you about how the drummer boy marches.
7 Where do you think the ambushers were hiding?
8 What does the writer say the army looks like?
9 Why do the men wave "secretly" at the drummer boy?
10 Write words you could use instead of these.

pennant (line 11)   struts (line 21)
sturdy (line 19)   glinting (line 12)
flecked (line 13)   tatters (line 33)

11 Leon Garfield, the author, uses many phrases which paint pictures in words:

"The hillside is in bloom with them." (line 2)
"Black spots on the complexion of the sky." (line 6)
"A sharp black shadow like a pit." (line 9)
"The drummer boy is their golden lad." (line 21)

Pick out those which you like and try to say why you like them. Write phrases of your own to describe the hillside; the wood; the birds in the sky; the banners.

The heron, the rook and the magpie

Rook

Heron

Magpie

Heron

The heron has grey and black wings; a grey and white neck; a yellow beak and a long black crest on its head. It is about 90 cms long. The heron hunts mainly in water but sometimes on land. It kills its prey by stabbing with its powerful beak. A small
5 creature or fish can be swallowed whole – a larger one is taken to the bank and eaten piece by piece. It eats fish, small birds, small mammals, insects and other creatures like snails, worms, lizards and frogs. Herons nest in colonies called heronries. There may be a few nests in a heronry or there may
10 be many. The nest is a large structure of twigs usually in the tops of trees. The eggs are laid in February to May with usually 3 – 5 in number. The eggs hatch in about a month but then it is about another seven weeks before the young are grown enough to leave the nest. The parents feed the young by
15 regurgitating food they have caught.

22

Rook

The rook is about 45 cms long. It is a glossy black colour with pale grey bare skin on its face at the base of its grey beak. It can be distinguished from other members of its family by the feathers around the tops of its legs. It nests in colonies in trees 5 and the number of nests in a colony can be from one or two to hundreds. The nests are rough structures of twigs. It eats a variety of creatures found on and in the ground — worms, insects and their larvae, small birds and mammals, grain and occasionally carrion (dead and rotting flesh). Sometimes 10 when it feeds in large numbers it can cause great damage. It lays between 3 and 5 greyish-blue eggs in March or April.

Magpie

This bird is about 45 cms long, of which about 20 − 25 cms are its tail. It is black and white in colour with glossy tinges of blue and green. It builds a domed roof over its nest in large bushes or trees. It eats insects, larvae, fruits, eggs, young and 5 small birds and carrion. The eggs are bluish-green and mottled in colour and usually six or more in number. The magpie is a great collector and stores away bright or glittering objects it finds.

Draw up a chart to show the information about these birds.

		Heron	Rook	Magpie
Size				
Food				
Eggs	colour			
	number			
Colour				
Nest	what it is like			
	where it is			
Distinguishing features				

Use your chart to answer these questions:-

1 Which bird has the most distinguishable colour?
2 Which bird might be considered a pest?
3 Which bird eats something the others do not? What is it?

23

The giant crab

A group of children set out to catch crabs from the pier.

Along the steep wall at the old pier's side,
The scavenging crabs come up with the tide.
"Want to catch one? It's easy! You don't need a thing
But a stone, and some fish, and some odd bits of string:
5   Look here now — I'll show you. First fetch that big stone —
The one with the hole through — the cobble-shaped one;
Now join up your string — all the odd bits you've got —
Loop one end through the stone, and tie tight in a knot;
Then cram in these bits of stale fish for a bait . . .
10 Ready? Over she goes!
       Now you've only to wait!"

Not long!

There's a tiny commotion below in the water:
There's a shout from above as the line becomes tauter;
15 There's a hauling up, hand over hand, until — whee-ee-ee!
A monster-great crab swings clear of the sea —
All legs and sharp claws, hanging desperately on,
His pincers stuck fast through the hole in the stone!
"Quick, get him!" "No hurry! He's stupid — he'll cling
20 Till we land him. Pull steady, and don't break the string.
Whoops! Over he comes! Give the string a sharp shake,
And he'll let go his hold and fall down on his back."

Well done!

"Now who'll pick him up?" "Not me!" "No, not me!
25 It's you said you fancied a crab for your tea!"
"I said? I don't want him!" "Hey, Billy, he's yours!
Come along and make friends with him!"
"What? With those claws?
I'm not touching him yet: I'll wait till he's dead!"

The Truants
John Walsh

1 What do you need to catch crabs?
2 What did they use for bait?
3 Describe in your own words how you prepare a line for catching crabs.
4 How do you get the crab off the line?
5 Why did the line become tauter (tight)?
6 Why didn't anyone want to pick the crab up?
7 How did the children feel when they first landed the crab?
8 How was the crab stuck to the stone?
9 What do you think will happen next?
10 Do you think this is a good poem? Give reasons for your answer.
11 Have you ever wanted to do something and not liked it afterwards? What was it?

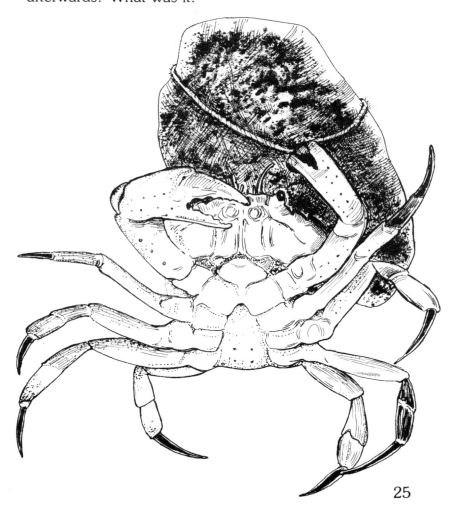

Lost in the mist

Rowena Farre goes to live with her aunt on a lonely farm in the north of Scotland. These small farms are called "crofts". She finds great joy in the animals there, particularly the grey seals which come to the rocky coast. There is hardship and danger too from the sudden changes in the weather.

A change had come over the sky since I had last taken note of it; the blue was not so intense and thin, vaporous clouds were forming. Down a cleft of the corrie blew a long streamer of mist. The sight of it made me double my pace. I
5   remembered then that I had come without a compass as I had not planned when setting out to go so high or so far. More and more clouds were forming in the sky and puffs of mist, less vaporous now, blew with increasing frequency into the corrie. There was always the possibility that a mist would disperse as
10 suddenly as it had come; on the other hand, it was equally possible for it to last hours or even days. I started to run, not as yet from any sense of panic, but because I realised it was important to reach the end of the corrie quickly and get a good view of my bearings. I was about five miles from home, high
15 up in the hills. As I started down the hill, keeping my eyes on the boulder − my immediate destination − and trying at the same time to avoid rocks and loose scree, the mist swept over the brow of the hill and enveloped me, blotting out every landmark and object excepting those within a few feet.
20   On walks with Ben I would often call "Home!" to him when the time came to retrace my steps, so that he would know I was returning. Now I spoke this word to him and trusted he would have the initiative to take upon himself the task of leading us back to the croft. For what seemed ages he
25 continued to sit without making a move.
        "Home!" I repeated urgently.
        At last he got up and with no sign of hurry began to walk forward; I followed, clinging to the lead as a drowning person might cling to a length of driftwood. We continued to walk

forwards at a slow pace. As the damp grasses flicked round my ankles I expected at any moment to sink into a swamp.

Seal Morning
Rowena Farre

1 How long might the mist have lasted?
2 Why did the writer start to run?
3 What did the writer expect to happen as she followed Ben?
4 How far was she away from home?
5 What were the first changes in the sky?
6 What had the writer forgotten to take with her?
7 What did Ben do on the first shout of "Home"?
8 Who or what was Ben?
9 Why do you think she kept her eyes on the boulder?
10 What do you think she had intended to do when she set out?
11 Write out the words from the lists which mean the same, or nearly the same, as the first word.

scree (line 17):   plants   small stones   bogs
    walls   boulders
intense (line 2):   interesting   frightening
very thick or strong   colourful   pretty
disperse (line 9):   give away   change
    move   find   spread out   disappear
corrie (line 8):   a hill   a hollow   a valley
    a hole   a peak

12 What do you think of this passage? Is it a good picture of being lost on the mountains in a mist? Does it make you feel anything for the writer? Give reasons for your anwers.
13 Have you ever been lost? If so, how did you feel? Did you feel anything like this writer?

Rose's lump

*Read the following passage. When you have read it make a
list of the best words you can think of to go in the blank
spaces.*

The morning started off quite normally, except that Rose
had a lump on her head.

"It's as . . .*1*. . . as an egg," said their father, gently feeling
it.

"Hm. A smallish . . .*2*. . . ." Louisa liked to be accurate.
Besides Rose was rather too proud . . .*3*. . . these things.
Japhet was right, it *would* be Rose who was . . .*4*. . . just
where the plaster fell. She was what Louisa had heard called
"accident-prone". If there was a . . .*5*. . . around, it stung
Rose; if there was a nail to sit on, . . .*6*. . . sat on it; if a log fell
off the logpile it would be sure to . . .*7*. . . on Rose. And a
toffee from the bag kept in the medicine cupboard was
. . .*8*. . . enough; Rose had a passion for First Aid. So
. . .*9*. . . hands, knees, heels and elbows were always either
covered with bits of frayed grey-pink Elastoplast, or rimmed
with . . .*10*. . . marks where the last piece had been. Her
record was three plasters, . . .*11*. . . bandages and a black
eyeshade for a stye.

"Can I go and show my lump to Mr and . . .*12*. . .
Gillings?"

"Don't swank," . . .*13*. . . Japhet. "Always wanting to be
petted."

"I'm *not*." And she scratched him with a . . .*14*. . . piece of
toast. Then Japhet dabbed her with an egg spoon, and
. . .*15*. . . had to be separated.

The Day the Ceiling Fell Down
Jennifer Wayne

Talk about the words you have chosen.

28

The black fox

Now try the same with this passage.

Tom has been sent to stay on a farm whilst his parents go abroad. He does not like the country and is missing his friends and life in the city. He is writing to his friend Petie telling him how boring everything is, when suddenly he sees a black fox.

I did not believe it for a minute, it was like my eyes were playing a trick or something, because I . . .*1*. . . just sort of staring across this field, thinking about my . . .*2*. . ., and then in the distance, where the grass was very . . .*3*. . ., I saw a fox leaping over the crest of a field. The grass . . .*4*. . . and the fox sprang towards the movement, and then, seeing that . . .*5*. . . was just the wind that had caused the grass to move, she . . .*6*. . .straight for the grove of trees where I was sitting.

It was so . . .*7*. . . that I wanted it to start over again, like you can turn movie film . . .*8*. . . and see yourself repeat some fine thing you have . . .*9*. . ., and I wanted to see the fox leaping over the grass . . .*10*. . .. In all my life I have never been so . . .*11*. . ..

I did not move at all, but I could . . .*12*. . . the paper in my hand shaking, and my heart seemed . . .*13*. . . have moved up in my body and got stuck in . . .*14*. . . throat.

The fox came straight towards the grove of . . .*15*. . ..She wasn't afraid, and I knew she had not . . .*16*. . . me against the tree. I stayed absolutely still even though I felt like . . .*17*. . . up and screaming, "Aunt Millie! Uncle Fred! Come see this. It's a . . .*18*. . ., a fox!"

The Midnight Fox
Betsy Byars

Talk about the words you have chosen.

More food please

These writers built a nest box and hid a camera at one end. A family of blue tits nested in the box, and the writers were able to watch their private world without disturbing them at all.

In their second week the young chicks grew to be much more active and bigger — and so did the caterpillars. At this age the hen began to leave the young on their own for short periods, and she went out to collect food for them along with
5 the cock. He had just found a fat caterpillar which curled like a green moustache around his beak. The cock's crest feathers were raised which showed that he was alarmed by something, perhaps a rival bird, which kept him from flying over to the nestbox. The hen was in a nearby tree stretching up to look all
10 around. She had a prize catch of two caterpillars in her beak.
The cock one day came in with the largest caterpillar we had yet seen. He tried to stuff it down a chick. The chick was willing, the cock tried patiently, but the caterpillar was winning. It refused to go down. Such a big caterpillar had jaws
15 which could cling to the mouth of the chick and we later often saw the parents bashing the bigger caterpillars on a tree branch to break their jaws or kill them before bringing them to the nest. But this caterpillar was lively. The cock gave up on chick number one, and was about to try his luck with another when
20 the hen entered and queued up behind him. He quickly took the opportunity to stand back and let her proceed while he held on to his uncooperative caterpillar. The hen hopped to the far side of the box and with immediate success fed her more dainty morsels to the chick with whom the cock had
25 failed.
Before she had a chance to move away, the cock leaned across, thrust his hefty grub into her beak, and himself made a hasty exit. He left her holding the nasty caterpillar, with not even a single interested customer in sight. The hen finally
30 solved the problem by using the cutting edge of her beak to divide the big meal into two more manageable portions, and

fed these separately to two chicks whose appetites had returned.

Window into a Nest
S. Morris and G. L. Flanagan

1 What was the chicks' main food?
2 How many chicks were in the nest?
3 How old were the chicks when their mother went out to look for food?
4 How did the hen solve the problem of the large caterpillar?
5 How did the writers know that the cock was alarmed?
6 Why could the cock not get the caterpillar down the chick's mouth?
7 Why did the cock give the hen the large caterpillar and then make "a hasty exit"?
8 What was the hen looking all around for (line 9)?
9 Write out any new things that this extract has told you about the feeding habits of blue tit chicks.
10 What does this passage tell you about the work of the parent birds?

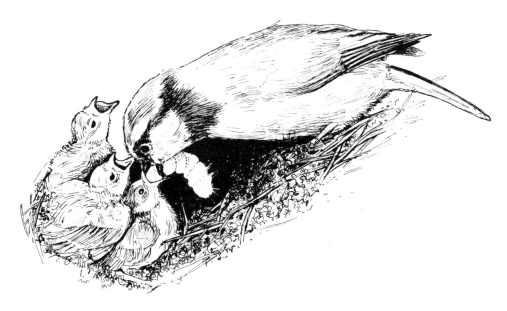

The hound fight

Drem lived many years ago, in what we call The Bronze Age. He wanted to become a warrior, but his right arm was useless. Nevertheless he determines to prove himself.

One night at a feast the men decide to have a dog fight to settle a quarrel. The King is choosing dogs for the fight. New Spears was a name for the young men of the tribe who are not yet warriors.

Now read on. The paragraphs are out of order, only the first one is done for you. Read them carefully, think about what is happening. Then put the paragraph letters in the order you think is correct.

A   At that unlucky moment, Whitethroat, standing beside Drem, flung up his head to nuzzle the boy's arm, in one of the sudden little bursts of affection that he was given to; and the firelight caught the silver blaze that had given him his name.

"So! That one!" the King said pointing. "That one with the white throat."

B   They were looking to him to thrust the dog forward. The pause could only have lasted a couple of heart beats, but it seemed to Drem to have dragged on for a hundred. And then, setting down the mead jar he still carried, he walked forward, with Whitethroat as usual pacing beside him, and turned, head thrown up, to face the King, to face Dumnorix his Chieftain and the big-bellied Bragon. He heard his own voice, loud and challenging, though his heart had lurched into the base of his throat. "We also, the New Spears, are called the Hounds of Dumnorix, and should we then have no part in this setting-on of hounds? Let one come out to me from among the New Spears who are the Hounds of Bragon, that we may fight it out here, beside the fire, for the third pair!"

C For one shocked instant of time, Drem did not believe it. It couldn't be Whitethroat he meant — not Whitethroat. But there was no mistaking the direction of the King's gaze and his pointing finger. Drem looked down at the great hound standing against his knee. Whitethroat's tail was swinging, and he gazed up at Drem trustingly, with amber eyes a little puzzled as though he caught the smell of something around him that he did not understand.

D There was a startled grunting, a startled rustle of voices round the fire. It was an unheard of thing that a boy who had not yet come to his Wolf Slaying should raise his voice in challenge before the Great Ones of the Tribe, before the King himself. But this challenge suited the wild humour of the assembled tribesmen none the less; and the King smote his knees with an open hand, laughing, "Well spoken, Hound of Dumnorix! And what say the Hounds of Bragon to that?"

E Drem looked at the other dog, the cunning, scarred veteran of many fights, his head lowered, the hackles already rising on his neck as though he understood perfectly what was expected of him; and in his eyes of red glint, the unmistakable red glint of the Killer. Whitethroat could fight when need arose, though he was no fighter by nature, but Drem knew with a sickening certainty that if they were matched together, Whitethroat would be killed because he himself was not a killer.

Warrior Scarlet
Rosemary Sutcliffe

The falcon's nest

The boy in this story runs away from home and sets up a home for himself in the mountains where his father used to have a farm. He lives alone, catching fish and other animals to eat. His greatest excitement is rearing and training a falcon.

I waited for the falcon patiently. I didn't have to go anywhere. After an hour or so, I was rewarded. A slender speck came from the valley and glided up the stream. It was still far away when it folded its wings and swooped down. I
5 watched. It arose, clumsy and big — carrying food — and winged back to the valley.

I sprinted down the stream and made myself a lean-to near some cliffs where I thought the bird had disappeared. Having learned that day that duck hawks prefer to nest on cliffs, I
10 settled for this site.

Early the next morning, I curled up behind a willow and watched the cliff.

The hawks came in from behind me and circled the stream. They had apparently been out hunting before I had got up, as
15 they were returning with food. This was exciting news. They were feeding young, and I was somewhere near the nest.

I watched one of them swing in to the cliff and disappear. A few minutes later, it winged out empty-footed. I marked the spot mentally and said, "Ha!"
20 After splashing across the stream in the shallows, I stood at the bottom of the cliff and wondered how on earth I was going to climb the sheer wall.

I wanted a falcon so badly, however, that I dug in with my toes and hands and started up. The first part was easy: it was
25 not too steep. When I thought I was stuck, I found a little ledge and shinned up to it.

I looked up to see how much higher I had to go when my hand touched something moist. I pulled it back and saw that it was white — bird droppings. Then I saw them. Almost where

30   my hand had been sat three fuzzy whitish-grey birds. Their wide open mouths gave them a startled look.

My Side of the Mountain
J. George

1 Where do duck hawks prefer to nest?
2 How long did the boy have to wait the first time?
3 Why was he so excited when he saw what the bird was carrying?
4 Why do you think he said "Ha!" when he did?
5 Where did he spend the night?
6 What told him he was near the nest?
7 Describe the young hawks in your own words.
8 Read the passage twice. Then write down all the words that tell you of the *movements* of the bird. The first word is "glided".

Now read the passage again and write the phrases that tell you what the boy did. The first one is "I waited".
9 Put these sentences in the order of the story.

I dug in with my toes and hands and started up.
Early next morning I watched the cliff.
I sprinted down to the stream to where the bird had disappeared.

10 What is a "lean-to"? What do you think this one looked like? Draw it if you like.

Points of view

A   Tabitha brought in a mouse
     "Good puss!" She curved with pride.
   Tabitha brought in a thrush.
     "You cruel cat!" we cried.

5 Tabitha, so sleek before,
     Now bristled as if to say:
   "Humans call us contrary!
     My whiskers! What are they?"

          Gilbert Thomas

B   Sometimes I share things,
10 And everyone says
   "Isn't it lovely? Isn't it fine?"

   I give my little brother
   Half my ice cream cone
   And let him play
15 With toys that are mine.

   But today
   I don't feel like sharing.
   Today
   I want to be let alone.
20 Today
   I don't want to give my little brother
   A single thing except
   A shove.

          Eve Merriam

1 What did Tabitha like to hunt?
2 How is the child in poem **B** kind to her brother?
3 What does Tabitha do when people call her "cruel cat"?
4 Look at poem **B**. When do people say "Isn't it fine?"?
5 Do you think Tabitha understood why the humans acted differently?
6 Do you think the little brother understood why the older child didn't always share?
7 Why does Tabitha think humans are contrary?
8 Why might the child sometimes want to give her little brother a shove?
9 How do you think the little brother feels when the older child doesn't feel like sharing or playing?
10 Find these words and write down what they mean in the passage.

   bristled (line 6)   contrary (line 7)
   share (line 9)   alone (line 19)
   single (line 22)

11 Why did people think differently about Tabitha's two killings? Write the answer you think best.
   (a) People are frightened of mice but not of birds.
   (b) Mice cause damage but birds don't.
   (c) Birds are prettier than mice.
   (d) Two-legged creatures shouldn't be hunted but four-legged can be.
   Talk about other reasons you can think of.
12 The little brother had done nothing 'wrong'. Talk about any time someone has behaved badly to you and you didn't know why.
13 Which poem do you like best and why?

The Great Hunger

In December 1846, an Irish Justice of the Peace wrote a letter to the Duke of Wellington. He had, he said, been surrounded by 200 starving peasants in a town in West Cork and had seen, "such frightful spectres as no man can imagine.
5 By far the greater number delirious, either from famine or from famine fever. Their demoniac yells are still ringing in my ears, and their horrible images are fixed upon my brain . . .."

This was the Great Hunger which struck Ireland in the mid-nineteenth century. Ireland at that time contained about eight
10 million people. Most were poor peasants, amongst the poorest in Europe. They worked tiny plots of land, and lived in windowless one-room mud cabins. In the south and west, they lived almost entirely on potatoes. They were large, tough potatoes, sometimes called "lumpers" or "horse potatoes".
15 In 1845, a fungus attacked the potato crop, and thrived in unusually damp weather. The blight spread quickly. Flourishing potato fields withered in a matter of days, becoming rotten, black and stinking of decay. In five or six months, the few potatoes from fields which had escaped had
20 been eaten. The Great Hunger began.

The next year was even worse. The entire crop failed. The Hunger became a mass famine with many deaths through starvation. People ate grass, refuse, even sawdust: their stomachs could not digest the meagre diet and diarrhoea set
25 in. Others were attacked in their weakened condition by famine fevers such as typhus. In the desperate search for food, even the closest family ties began to break down. One country doctor wrote, "I have seen mothers snatch food from the hands of their starving children; known a father engage in
30 a mortal struggle with a son for a potato."

Disasters
Macdonald

1 What did the Irish peasants normally mainly live on?
2 What other names were given to potatoes?
3 Who wrote to the Duke of Wellington?
4 Which part of Ireland was he describing?
5 What was the weather like during 1845 in Ireland?
6 What did the fields look like after the blight had struck?
7 How was the year 1846 worse than 1845?
8 Describe in your own words the ways of life of the Irish peasants before the famine.
9 Why was the failure of the potato crop so serious for the Irish peasants?
10 *Either* write out the meanings of these words, *or* write words you could use in their place.

      spectres (line 4)   famine (line 5)
      thrived (line 15)   withered (line 17)
      meagre (line 24)   mortal (line 30)

11 From what the passage tells you, write out the best answer to the questions below.
Why did fevers spread so quickly?
(a) Because there were no doctors.
(b) Because the people were weak through starvation.
(c) Because germs spread quickly.
Why did potato disease thrive?
(a) Because they only had small plots of land.
(b) Because they only grew potatoes.
(c) Because they were not good farmers.
(d) Because the weather was wet.
Why did members of families fight each other?
(a) Because they didn't like each other.
(b) To get what little food there was.
(c) Because the fever drove them mad.
12 What do you think it must have been like for the children of the Irish peasants?
13 What do you think could have been done to help the Irish peasants?

The ducking

"Duck him in the canal, then," Moses said. "Make him drink it. That'll give him a belly ache he won't forget in a hurry."

5 Adam shifted his grasp and twisted Philip's right arm up behind him, forcing him down on his knees on the edge of the canal, pushing his head down. Philip saw a dead fish floating, silver and slimy, and twisted his face away. "There's worse than dead fish, Your Royal Highness," Moses said in a sepulchral voice. "There's corpses in there, dead men with no
10 eyes."

"Please," Philip begged, "please don't, please . . ." — but Adam's hand pushed hard on the back of his neck and his face went down, into the water. He closed his eyes and held his breath until it seemed his lungs were bursting. They yanked
15 his head up, by his hair, let him gulp air for a second, then shoved him down again. This time the water went up his nose and down his throat and he thought he was drowning. He wriggled and thrashed, and, when they let him go suddenly, nearly fell into the water. He grabbed the concrete side of the
20 canal and pulled himself back to safety, choking and retching. Drums banged in his ears; then a loud, hollow slapping. When he had stopped being sick, he raised his head dizzily and saw that Moses had disappeared and that Adam was flat on his back on the tow path with someone kneeling on top of him
25 and hitting him, open-handed, first on one side of his face and then on the other. Philip blinked. He said, "Darcy!" and got to his feet. He saw blood on Adam's face and his eyes open and staring. Philip said, terrified, "Darcy, don't . . ."

Darcy stopped hitting Adam. He stood up and kicked him.
30 He said, "Get up, filthy slob."

The Robbers
Nina Bawden

40

1 How did Adam force Philip down?
2 How did Philip get back to safety?
3 Where was Adam when Philip came to his senses?
4 What did Philip first see in the canal?
5 How was Philip feeling as they began to push his head in?
6 Write out the words that tell you what Philip *did* the second time his head was pushed in.
7 Who do you think Darcy was?
8 Who do you think Adam and Moses were?
9 Why do you think Adam called Philip "Your Royal Highness"?
10 Why do you think they let him go suddenly?
11 Why was Philip "terrified" when he saw Darcy slapping Adam?
12 Look at these words in the passage:
   sepulchral (line 9); yanked (line 16); retching (line 20).
   Which of these meanings fits each word?

   pulled with a jerk
   gloomy, dismal
   vomiting; being sick
13 Look at the phrases "Drums banged in his ears" (line 21) and "he raised his head dizzily" (line 22). Are these good phrases? What do they tell you? Can you think of phrases of your own for these feelings?

The bus stop

Read this passage and draw a sketch of what it tells you.

When Martin reached the bus stop sign at the edge of the
kerb just away from the corner of Hill Road, he was
disappointed to find six people already waiting in a queue,
though two of them were children and, he thought, probably
5 wouldn't count if the bus conductor wasn't too fussy. Still the
man reading the newspaper just on the other side of the sign
worried him. Was he in the queue or not?

He was glad to put down his tackle box, which seemed to
be getting heavier, and lean his rod against the tree growing
10 up through the pavement.

The thin man at the head of the line had put down his brief
case as if it, too, were heavy, but he kept it safely between his
legs. He was anxiously keeping an eye on the toddler in the
push-chair, who was waving an ice-cream about dangerously
15 near his neat trousers. The toddler's mother was leaning on
the push-chair reading a magazine, totally ignoring the child
and the ice-cream.

Martin looked at the stout woman next to him and
wondered why she didn't put down her two bulging shopping
20 bags. She was talking to the postman just in front of her,
though he didn't seem to be listening. He was busy keeping
his bag out of the way of the toddler's older brother, who kept
poking his finger into a little hole at the bottom of the bag.

Martin was very relieved when he saw Phil approaching,
25 because then he thought, at least we'll be late together if we
can't get on this bus.

S. Ashworth

42

The way to freedom

Robin is a crippled boy who has escaped from a castle under siege to raise help. He is not sure which way to go.

The path led through a wood and downward toward the valley of a stream which joined the one surrounding the castle. There were no cottages near at hand, but across the stream and beyond a low-lying field and a rising slope Robin could
5   see the wood that extended to the edge of the village where the church tower stood. The sky was filled with fast-flying clouds and the fog was gone. The stream was shallow enough for Robin to go across on foot and the little wetting he got was nothing after swimming the river.
10   The wood behind him hid Robin from the camp in the field, for which he was thankful, because the rising ground slowed his going, and he felt as if he were a fair target for arrows. It seemed as if he would never come to the top of the field and the hedgerow separating it from the forest beyond. When he
15   reached the shelter of the great trees, Robin sank down into a bed of bracken to rest. He was very tired.

The Door in the Wall
M. de Angeli

1   Draw a sketch of the place where Robin is.
2   What is Robin doing in the extract?
3   Can you say whether there was any danger in Robin's journey? What reasons have you for your answer?
4   There is one word in the passage that gives you a clue about when the story takes place. Find the word and make a guess about when the story takes place.
5   Talk with your friends about your sketches and the reasons you gave for question 4.

At the fair

Miss Oxley, the teacher, has taken Peter and his friends to the fair.

Miss Oxley pressed his hand and they stopped at the edge of the fair, and the noise of it came running up to them like the waves of the sea, bursting and receding. "It does sound ugly," Miss Oxley said. "Don't you think it sounds ugly?"

5 The voices of the barkers and the side-show attendants were raucous and singsong. "Seven balls for sixpence! Over twenty-one and win a prize!" "Three darts for sixpence. Three darts for sixpence! Score the lucky number and win a prize!" "Three shies for sixpence! Win a coconut or pick a prize!"

10 "They're all saying, 'Give us your money quick and go away!' " Peter said, "in different dialects."

Miss Oxley laughed. "You're too sharp. You hear what people mean."

There was something in all this, the noise of the steam-
15 organ and the whirr of the switchback and the grind of the roundabout and the screams and the shouts and the chatter and the banging of the dodgem cars and the ping of the bullets striking the metal plate at the back of the booth and the baby crying and the woman saying, "And I said to her, Mrs Amies, I
20 said. . . ." and the rattle of metal wheels on metal rails and the high voices chanting "Seven balls for sixpence. Win a prize and win a prize and win a prize!" which was ugly and strident and all mixed up and yet excited him. "Let's just walk round," Peter said. "Let's listen!"

25 Then he thought Rose Oxley might want something else, she might want to pay sixpence and win a prize. "That is, if you don't mind," he said.

They went to the centre of the fair and stood between the merry-go-round and the dodgem cars in what appeared an
30 inferno of noise, of banging, grinding, screaming, chanting, roaring. Peter Ambrose stood with his face lifted up to the sky

and his eyes closed, listening to what appeared to Miss Oxley an ear-splitting babel of sounds.

The Fair to Middling
A. C. Marshall

1 Did Miss Oxley like the sound of the fair?
2 What noises could be heard from the dodgems?
3 Which two places did they stand at?
4 What did Peter say the voices and cries all meant? Do you think he was right in what he thought?
5 What did Peter want to do?
6 Why does Miss Oxley think Peter is too sharp?
7 Why do you think Miss Oxley pressed Peter's hand?
8 Who are "the barkers"? Do you think this is a good name for the job they do? Why?
9 Write down which of these words fits Peter.

    clever   kind   sad   thoughtful   happy

10 Pick out the right meaning for these words.

    dialect (line 11): voices   language   ways sounds
    inferno (line 30): scene of horror   blazing fire bedlam   a background
    raucous (line 6): musical   very clear   quiet harsh voiced
    strident (line 22): sweet   loud and shrill   soft unclear   bossy
    receding (line 3): moving   making a noise going back   calling out

11 Does this passage give a good description of the sounds you have heard at a fair?
12 Peter Ambrose was blind. Which parts of the passage give you a clue about this?

    Which of his other senses was very keen? Is this usual with blind people?

Elephants are different to different people

This passage tells the different thoughts three people had when they saw an elephant at the zoo.

Wilson and Pilcer and Snack stood before the zoo elephant.

Wilson said, "What is its name? Is it from Asia or Africa? Who feeds it? Is it a he or a she? How old is it? Do they have twins? How much does it cost to feed? How much does it
5   weigh? If it dies, how much will another one cost? If it dies, what will they use the bones, the fat, and the hide for? What use is it besides to look at?"

Pilcer didn't have any questions; he was murmuring to himself, "It's a house by itself, walls and windows, the ears
10   come from tall cornfields, by God; the architect of those legs was a workman, by God; he stands like a bridge out across deep water; the face is sad and the eyes are kind; I know elephants are good to babies."

Snack looked up and down and at last said to himself, "He's
15   a tough son-of-a-gun outside and I'll bet he's got a strong heart, I'll bet he's strong as a copper-riveted boiler inside."

They didn't put up any arguments.
They didn't throw anything in each other's faces.
Three men saw the elephant three ways
20   And let it go at that.
They didn't spoil a sunny Sunday afternoon;
"Sunday comes only once a week," they told each other.

Carl Sandburg

1 Wilson, Pilcer and Snack see the elephant very clearly. What were each one's main ideas?

2 Why didn't the three men argue about their views of an elephant?

3 Do you think they enjoyed themselves at the zoo? Why?

How to talk to elephants

I was following the crest of a ridge along one of the many old elephant trails that criss-crossed the bamboo. Soon the tracks became fresh. The toe-nails were still clearly defined, and swarms of tiny black flies hovered about the heaps of dung. I pushed my fingers into some dung. It was still warm. Clouds drifted in, and grey fog crept from stem to stem, reducing my visibility to about fifty feet. I continued silently and carefully, straining my senses, trying to see the bulky grey forms of the elephants in this shadowless, dusky world, trying to smell their musky odour. But the only sound was the pounding of my heart. I was afraid of stumbling upon the herd, for it would be dangerous to have to elude them in this fog. Finally I talked to them in a normal voice: "Elephants, hallo. Please get off the trail. This ridge leads to my camp, and I don't want to leave it. I am only a human being, a weakling without weapons. I can do you no harm. Please leave the trail and let me pass." And just ahead, without a sound, the elephants left the trail and angled into the valley.

G. B. Schaller

Use both passages to answer these questions.
1 What did the man try to listen for?
2 How did he know that the elephants were near?
3 Why could he not follow the tracks so well?
4 What does this passage tell you about (a) the smell of elephants; (b) the tracks they make; (c) how they might answer prayers?
5 Where do these elephants live? In what ways are they different from those in the passage opposite?
6 Who do you think really knows more about elephants, Schaller or the men in Sandburg's passage?
7 Do the men in each passage like elephants or not? Give reasons for your answer.

First published in 1982 by Basil Blackwell Limited
Reprinted in 1982, 1983, 1985, 1987, 1988, 1990, 1991

Reprinted in 1992, 1993, 1994 by
Simon & Schuster Education

Reprinted in 1994 by
Stanley Thornes (Publishers) Ltd
Ellenborough House
Wellington Street
CHELTENHAM GL50 1YW
England
Reprinted in 1995

A catalogue record for this book is available from the British Library.

ISBN 0 7487 1964 4

Acknowledgements

We are grateful to the following for permission to reproduce copyright material: Atheneum Publishers for "Sometimes" from Catch a Little Rhyme by Eve Merriam; David and Charles for "Point of View" from Collected Poems by Gilbert Thomas; Faber and Faber Ltd for "Roman Wall Blues" from Collected Shorter Poems by W. H. Auden; the author for "Spring" from The Sparrow Bush by Elizabeth Coatsworth; Harcourt Brace Jovanovich for an extract from The Complete Poems of Carl Sandburg; Mrs A. M. Walsh for "The Giant Crab" from The Truants by John Walsh; Curtis Brown Ltd, London, on behalf of the Estate of Ogden Nash for "Winter Morning" from The New Nutcracker Suite and other innocent verses by Ogden Nash.

Typesetting by Getset (BTS) Ltd, Eynsham, Oxford

Printed in Hong Kong by Wing King Tong Co. Ltd.